## SUPERBASE 23
# SEYMOUR JOHNSON

# SUPERBASE 23

# SEYMOUR JOHNSON

## Eagles, Chiefs and Rocketeers

### Mark R Wagner

OSPREY
AEROSPACE

# Acknowledgements

The photos in this book could not have been obtained without the generous assistance offered to the author by the following individuals: Brigadier General J O McFalls III, 4th TFW Commander; Lt Col Rusty Bolt, 336th TFS Commander; Lt Col Robert Gruver; Lt Col Steve Pingel, 335th TFS Commander; MSgt Rodney Anthony, 336th AMU; SMSgt Richard VanHook, 4th TFW AMT; MSgt Charles Nichols, 4th TFW AMT; MSgt Ross Hunter, 191st FIG; CMSgt Joshua Chadwick III, 4th TFW MOD; MSgt George Strunk, Chief Base Weather Ops (for all the good weather when needed); 1st Lt David Disipio, ATC Ops; Capt Mark Alred, 336 TFS; Mr Doyle Payne, F-15E simulator manager, Loral Defense Systems; Mr Tom Cantrell, F-4E simulator; Lt Col Gail Tatum, Asst Dep Commander for Maintenance, 68th AREFW; Capt Edward Breen, 68th AREFW; Capt Shaun Kelleher, 68th AREFW; Sgts Holt, Holland, Walden, Black and Airman Gardner, engine test shop; and Justin Russell for accommodation. Finally Mr Jay Barber, Assistant Chief Public Affairs Division and SrA Luke Britt for their patience and time.

Published in 1991 by Osprey Publishing Limited
59 Grosvenor Street, London W1X 9DA

© Mark R Wagner

British Library Cataloguing in Publication Data
Wagner, Mark R.
  Seymour Johnson. – (Superbase, 23).
  1. United States. Military aircraft
  I. Title II. Series
  358.4170973

ISBN 1-85532-173-4

Written and edited by Tony Holmes
Page design by Paul Kime
Printed in Hong Kong

**Front cover** Whilst his Phantom II suckles away on JP4, the pilot keeps a firm fix on the KC-10 Extender's flying boom as it towers over him. The boom's fly-by-wire wings can just be seen in reflection on his visor. En route to bomb a live range on Naval Air Station (NAS) Roosevelt Roads, Puerto Rico, this F-4E was one of four aircraft despatched by the 334th Tactical Fighter Squadron (TFS) on *Exercise Caribbean Eagle II*

**Back cover** Screwdriver at the ready, a maintainer sets about fixing a minor glitch within the avionics bay of a 336th TFS F-15E Strike Eagle

**Title page** Fuel streams from the probe as the McDonnell Douglas Advanced Aerial Refuelling Boom (AARB) breaks contact with the F-4E's receptacle during a JP4 exchange over the Caribbean. Immediately aware of the break, the Phantom II pilot from the 334th Tactical Fighter Squadron (TFS) peers up through the canopy and attempts to manoeuvre his 25-ton mount back into the correct position

**Right** 'Now where did I leave my lunch pail?' An anonymous technician from the now defunct 68th Air Refueling Wing (ARW) comes to grips with the KC-10's substantial nose gear strut. The serial '0123' on the gear door denotes that this airframe (87–0123) is the youngest, bar one, of the 20-strong KC-10 fleet at Seymour Johnson

For a catalogue of all books published by Osprey Aerospace please write to:

**The Marketing Department, Octopus Illustrated Books, 1st Floor, Michelin House, 81 Fulham Road, London SW3 6RB**

This book is dedicated to Major Peter S Hook and Captain James B Poulet, 335th TFS, and Lieutenant Colonel Donnie R Holland and Major Thomas F Koritz, 336th TFS, all of whom made the ultimate sacrifice in the fight to liberate Kuwait

# Introduction

An old and proud facility steeped in tradition, the sprawling base that is today's Seymour Johnson has its roots firmly planted in the dark days of World War 2. Activated in June 1942 as just one of the many fledgling training fields built by the Army Air Service to help the Allied war effort cope with the Axis onslaught in Europe and Asia, Seymour Johnson trained many a fighter pilot over the next three years.

Sited within the city limits of Goldsboro, North Carolina, the base owes its name to a native of the area, Navy Lieutenant Seymour Andrew Johnson, who was killed in an air crash in Maryland on 5 March 1941.

As with many of the new bases established during the war, Seymour Johnson was deactivated soon after the conflict ended. Closed for almost a decade, the facility was restored to flying stations on 1 April 1956, the 83rd Fighter (Day) Wing taking up a short term of residence. This unit was soon replaced by the famous 4th Fighter (Day) Wing the following year. Resident ever since, the 'Fighting Fourth' are still to be found amongst the firs in North Carolina today, albeit now as the first of USAF's new 'composite wings' encompassing both Tactical and Strategic Air Command assests under the control of TAC. Go back 50 years, however, to the green fields of eastern England and you will find the origins of the former 4th TFW in a trio of Royal Air Force Eagle Squadrons. Staffed by volunteer American pilots, No 71, No 121 and No 133 Sqns flew alongside other RAF units in the tense years of 1941–42, before joining the USAAF's 8th Air Force in the latter half of 1942. Redesignated the 4th Fighter Group, the wing continued to serve in Europe up until war's end.

The late 1940s saw the wing back in America transitioning initially onto the F-80 Shooting Star and then the F-86 Sabre. Called to arms yet again in November 1950, the 4th became the first Sabre-equipped outfit committed to the Korean War. Over the next three years pilots from the wing wrote for themselves a special place in the aviation history books as they proceeded to decimate the Communist MiG-15 force, shooting down no fewer than 502 enemy aircraft (52 per cent of the overall Allied total). Twenty-four 4th FW pilots achieved ace status in the process.

The following decade saw the wing move to Seymour Johnson and transition onto the F-100 Super Sabre, quickly followed by the F-105 Thunderchief. Sent to Vietnam in1965, the wing bade farewell to the Thunderchief two years later and embraced the Phantom II in return. Veterans of no fewer than 8000 combat sorties during the war years, the 4th eventually returned home in 1973. Trading up to the F-4E in 1980, the wing continued their long tradition as 'Phantom Phlyers' up until December 1990 when the final F-4Es from the 334th departed Seymour Johnson for Texas.

The first in F-15Es and the first of the new 'composite wings', the 4th has also recently added further battle honours to its impressive list of achievements. Both the 335th and 336th TFSs flew in excess of 10,000 combat hours during Operation Desert Storm in January and February 1991.

Seymour Johnson has experienced several major changes over the past five years but the recent reshuffling of equipment and structure has made the base a key facility in the Air Force's future, both in continental America and abroad.

# Contents

**Above** As is standard with USAF fighter units, the flagship of the 335th TFS wears drop shadow tailcodes and full squadron titling on its twin fins. Each fighter unit within the 4th Wing adorns one of its aircraft in this fashion, the wing CO's F-15E going one step further with a representative badge from all three squadrons worn on its left intake

# The Aged Warrior

With the EOR (end of runway) checks completed, it's 'chocks away' for this F-4E (73–0160) of the 334th TFS. Phantom II-equipped since 1967, the 'Eagles' built up an enviable reputation on the F-4D during the hardest years of the Vietnam conflict. The dayglo-jacketed airman with the headset on isn't trying to hitch a lift with the crew – he is signalling to his partner that it's safe to clear away from the growling F-4. The cord running across the shimmering ramp plugs into a communication socket just forward of the intake, allowing the 'groundie' to talk to the crew, and vice versa

**Left** With all obstructions removed and the groundcrew now safely sheltering from both the sun and the noise in their line shed, the pilot takes one more look at the dials before receiving clearance from the tower to commence taxying. Beneath the wings are a pair of triple ejector racks (TERs) loaded with 25 1b 'blue' bombs, the USAF's favoured training device

**Above** Clearance received, the pilot eases off the brakes, blips the throttle, and heads out towards the 'black top', both J79s rumbling purposefully behind him. Having checked the comms and primed the APQ-120 radar, the weapons system officer (WSO) just sits back and tries to keep cool during the slow roll out. From this angle all the special mods, which were progressively fitted to the late-build E-models, can be clearly seen. The wider, Navy-style, leading-edge slats are fully deployed, and at the root of the wing the spherical fairing which contains the Target Identification System Electro-Optical (TISEO) device juts out alongside the intake. Finally, beneath the radome the black panelling forward of the gun fairing denotes the fitment of the long-barrelled version of the ubiquitous M61A1 20 mm cannon. Fitted beneath the intake is a Westinghouse AN/ALQ-131 noise and deception electronic countermeasures (ECM) pod, a vital 'bolt-on extra' that was carried by virtually all F-4Es during their final days in North Carolina

Surrounded by the lush green forest that covers much of North Carolina, a
lightly laden 'Eagle' taxies out toward the EOR ramp at the threshold of runway
26. Here, the red-flagged safety pins will be removed from the ordnance and
the Phantom II will be cleared for departure. Visible behind the aircraft is the
diminutive base control tower

Captured just at the point of rotation, F-4E 72–0124 rockets down the tarmac with its twin J79-GE-17A turbojets on full military power. Besides the mandatory 600 US gal centreline tank and the AN/ALQ-131 ECM pod, this aircraft also carries a single Ford Aerospace AIM-9N Sidewinder round on its port inboard pylon. As with the centre tank, these pylons are always present under the wings of the F-4 and can carry both a TER and a pair of Sidewinders flanking the ordnance

**Above** Cruising down over the Turks and Caicos Islands, southbound at 20,000 ft and 300 kts, heading for a bombing raid on the island of Puerto Rico. Here 73–0172 approaches the KC-10A for a fuel top up before commencing the final phase of the sortie. Although the boom is flown into position by the aerial refuelling operator (ARO) aboard the tanker, the responsibility lies with the pilot to correctly position his aircraft behind the KC-10 in the first place, thus making the 'boomers' life far less complicated

**Right** Loaded with six 500 lb Mk 82 'iron' bombs, the F-4E delicately approaches the boom. From this head-on angle, the beautifully tapered semi-coke bottle rule fuselage of the classic St Louis fighter is shown to advantage

**Above** All topped up, the F-4E slides away from the tanker to start its attacking descent to 1000 feet at high speed. The targets at NAS Roosevelt Roads on Vieques Island, Puerto Rico, are an ammo dump, hardened aircraft shelters and a missile site. During *Operation Desert Storm*, the then 4th TFW (now fully equipped with F-15Es) flew sorties against live targets in Iraq and Kuwait, delivering their ordnance at ceilings down to 500 feet. Although flying a much more capable aircraft into combat, the 4th benefited significantly from the many years of experience gained with the F-4, particularly when it came to the accurate delivery of dumb bombs

**Left** With the magnetic-ended boom linked up, the JP4 automatically flows. The pilot's eyes at this moment are firmly fixed on the traffic light indicator panel immediately in front of the boom. This visual aid, plus the detailed yellow 'snail trails' beneath the tanker's fuselage, enable the pilot to position his aircraft in exactly the right patch of sky in any weather, day or night, in total radio silence

**Left** Home to over 65 aircraft, the ramp at Seymour Johnson is liberally covered with USAF hardware, this line being just one of three that darkens the pale concrete. Inspiring in peace time, these impressive lines would be of little use to anyone, save a ground hugging enemy pilot, during war

**Below** Get in close to a Phantom II and the flush-rivetted skin of the aircraft clearly shows up, the formerly sleek machine taking on the appearance of a metallic 'patchwork' quilt. Although nearing its twentieth birthday, this airframe is not suffering a late-life crisis as it has been maintained in immaculate condition by the 334th Aircraft Maintenance Unit (AMU)

**Above** Fused and ready for loading, the Mk 82 500 lb bombs are carefully driven into position by squadron armourers. The live weapons loading area is rendered totally sterile by the armourers during a human chain search of the tarmac for foreign object debris prior to the ordnance arriving

**Left** Exposing its M61A1 breech to the late afternoon sun, F-4E 73–0172 is checked over by a line technician in preparation for an early morning sortie the following day. As can be seen from this shot, a purpose-built cover has been snugly fitted over the forward antenna of the AN/ALQ-131 pod, thus stopping moisture from seeping into the highly sensitive avionics

**Above** You don't want the clutch to slip when you're in this position! Having carefully manoeuvred his MJ-1 munitions loader beneath the port pylon, the driver keeps a close eye on proceedings. The MJ-1, or 'jammer' as it is known in the air force, is a ubiquitous design that is found on USAF bases across the globe. Powered by a diesel engine, the MJ-1 can carry bombs, missiles or ECM pods, various loading heads slotting into the arms to accommodate the circumference of the ordnance being uplifted

**Right** With the bombs firmly attached and the 'jammer' out of the way, the armourers give the Mk 82s the final once-over before declaring the F-4 mission ready. Triple ejector racks (TER) have been hung under various American warplanes since the late 1950s, the design being of a standard NATO size to allow it to carry ordnance of various extractions

Now just awaiting its crew, F-4E 74–0649 sits silently on the loading ramp, the entry ladder strategically positioned behind the nose gear. This airframe was one of six 334th TFS Phantom IIs bombed-up for the *Caribbean Eagle II* sortie. Of the six, only four F-4s actually undertook the mission, two airframes being prepared as spares in case of a problem rendering the primary Phantom IIs unserviceable during the preflights

The 'front office' for the 4th TFW pilots for over 25 years. Representing early '60s switchology at its best, the F-4E simulator at Seymour Johnson has changed very little since it was installed at the base over a decade ago. Having trained innumerable pilots in the art of 'Phlying' the F-4, the well-used simulator was finally deactivated and removed in the summer of 1990

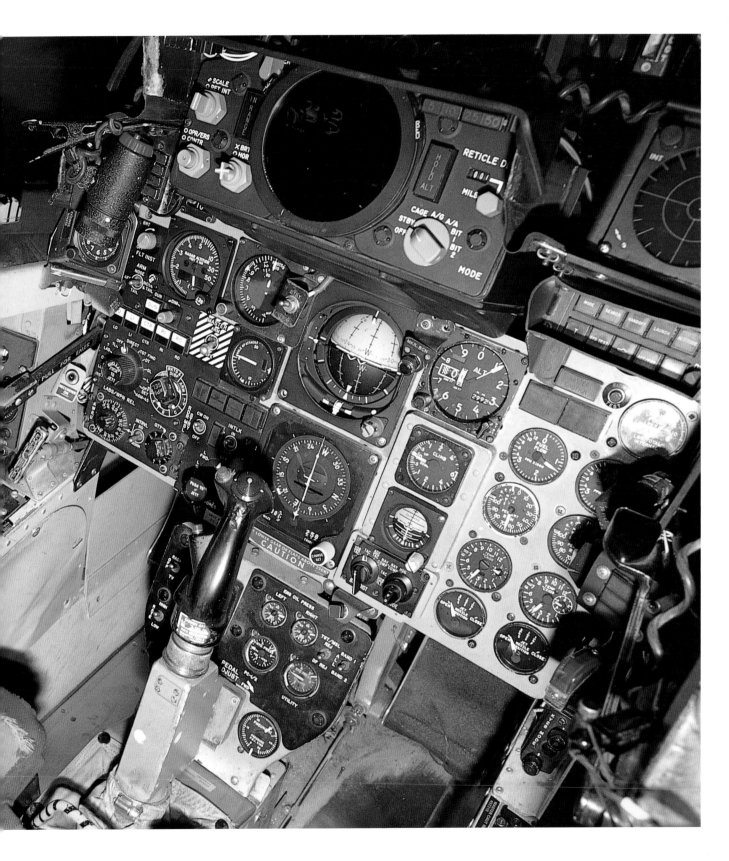

Just as the front office hasn't changed much over the decades, neither have things back aft, the Weapon's Systems Officers' (WSO) simulator looking virtually identical to the layout fitted in the F-4Cs of 25 years ago. The glowing scope in the centre of the console indicates the targets that are being tracked by the aircraft's Westinghouse APQ-120 radar fire control system. Being very late-build airframes in the overall Phantom II programme, the Wing's F-4s benefited from redesigned 'ergonometric' instrumentation, thus making the crew's job marginally easier, particularly in a combat scenario

**Above** Undergoing a periodic inspection, 72–0139 was soon passed fit for service and returned to the ranks of the 334th. Aside from the prominent tailhook resting on the tarmac, the hinged dragchute door has also been cranked open for inspection. Items like these are not regularly used during the course of a typical mission and therefore have to be checked on the ground to ensure their operational status

**Left** Chocked and tagged, a visiting F-4E points into the rising sun on Seymour Johnson's transient ramp. Besides carrying a full load of external tanks, the aircraft has a small travel pod bolted to the port hardpoint. The crews usually fill these pods with golf clubs, tennis racquets and overnight bags, as the internal storage space for personal effects is not overgenerous in the F-4. Across the tarmac, the wing of a visiting B-52 stretches out as the bomber relaxes before departing on the next leg of its journey

**Above** Whilst the J79s sit quietly, the base locale is filled with the sounds of two Pratt & Whitney F100s on military power, propelling a 'clean' Strike Eagle skyward. The 334th TFS finally traded in their last F-4E in December 1990, commencing work-ups with the potent new F-15E soon after

**Right** Fighting a losing battle, the F-4s are all but submerged in a 'forest' of twin tails. Parked alongside the 'bossman's' machine is the very last Phantom II delivered to the USAF, this particular airframe having been collected by the 4th TFW from the McDonnell Douglas plant at St Louis over 15 years ago

The 4th TFW's F-4Es were old, but not as old as the clutch of Delta models that lived on permanent Zulu alert down near the threshold of runway 26. Fulfilling a long standing duty to the USAF, the Air National Guard provides several key airbases on the east and west coasts with 24-hour air defence. Regularly tasked with performing this vital function, the Michigan Air Guard's 171st Fighter Interceptor Squadron (FIS) have been a colourful part of everyday life at Seymour Johnson for well over a decade. With its canopies cranked back and intake covers firmly in place, F-4D 66–0254 takes a break from quick reaction alert duty. The aircraft wears an unusual Europe One camouflage scheme, which on a combat air patrol would no doubt stand out like the proverbial sore thumb! Finally retired from service at the end of 1990, this weary veteran of the Vietnam War now spends its days permanently soaking up the sun in Arizona at the Davis-Monthan boneyard

Besides the almost mandatory Phantom II gate guard at the entrance to the 4th TW's headquarters, the only remaining F-4 at Seymour Johnson is this worn-out Charlie model, which serves as a training tool for the Battle Damage Repair Section of the 4th Equipment Maintenance Squadron (EMS). Although now liberally patched up and generally scruffy in appearance, the old warrior still proudly wears the last vestiges of its air defence grey scheme. Contrary to the 'SJ' tailcodes sprayed on the fin, this aircraft actually finished its days with the 123rd FIS, Oregon ANG, at Portland International Airport. The unit now flies the rather more potent F-15A Eagle

**Right** Day or night, with no shutdowns for holidays, the 171st detachment is on constant standby to scramble – usually to intercept Soviet Air Force Tupolev Tu-142 *Bear* reconnaissance aircraft inside, or approaching, US airspace. Here Captain Pete Benson (pilot), Major Bob McCarthy (WSO) and SSgt Ed Albright pose by the hangared, but ready to go, F-4D 66–0279. Beneath the F-4, the powercart hose and auxiliary generator leads trail away to their respective installations, the aircraft's avionics being fully fired up at all times. Rather surprisingly, the Phantom II's armament consists of just a pair of AIM-7F Sparrows

**Above** Hangared alongside '0279 is 65–0704, one of the oldest F-4Ds on the squadron books. Looking resplendent in its air defence Egypt One greys, this old warrior wears the traditional chequers and chevrons so long associated with the 171st, although only as shades of grey instead of the more colourful yellow and black. Always in fighters, the unit's history dates way back to 374th Fighter Squadron, which flew Mustangs and Thunderbolts with the Eighth Air Force in Europe during World War 2. Renumbered and reassigned to the Air Guard on 25 April 1948, the unit commenced operations with F-51Ds at the Detroit-Wayne Major Airport soon after. Embracing jet power in the form of the Republic F-84B Thunderjet two years later, the 171st was called to active duty and sent to Luke AFB, Arizona, to help train pilots converting onto type to make up the numbers during the Korean War. Briefly flirting with the F-51 (H-models) yet again, the 171st finally replaced the piston-engined classic with the F-86E Sabre in November 1953. At the time the unit was tasked with air defence duties, the all-weather F-89C Scorpion replacing the 'fine weather' Sabre in June 1955. A change of role saw the 171st transition on to the RF-84F Thunderflash in February 1958, the unit retaining the rugged Republic reconnaissance aircraft until being replaced by the equally tough RF-101A/C Voodoo in January 1971. With the 'new' Voodoos came a change of residence, the squadron moving to Selfridge Air National Guard Base. The RF-101s did not last long however, as the unit was once more tasked with air defence duties, the 171st Tactical Reconnaissance Squadron becoming the 171st Fighter Interceptor Squadron accordingly. Equipped with the gracious F-106 Delta Dart by July 1972, the unit began its relationship with Seymour Johnson soon afterwards. F-4Cs replaced the F-106s in 1978, and the Deltas took over from the Charlies in the mid-1980s. Having operated all manner of jets over the past four decades, the 171st finally got their hands on some relatively modern equipment in December 1990 when the first of 20 F-16As arrived at Selfridge. Although initially equipped with basic Alpha models, the 171st are having their baseline aircraft upgraded to Air Defense Fighter (ADF) specs, thus making the Fighting Falcon the perfect interceptor for the 'Guard

# 'Chiefs' and 'Rocketeers'

**Left** Surrounded by the general clutter of the modern ramp, nine F-15Es of the 336th TFS are prepared for the day's sorties. Behind the closest aircraft, two trolleys laden with live Mk 82 500 lb Snakeye retarded bombs await the arrival of the amourers. Emphasizing the Strike Eagle's dual role, four AIM-7F Sparrows and a trio of AIM-9L Sidewinders also sit on their racks prior to being uplifted onto the aircraft. As with the bombs, these rounds are all blue striped, which signifies that they are 'live' and to be treated with due respect. Indicating just how new these F-15Es are, the closest airframe has yet to receive the stencilled name of its allocated plane captain in the stylized rectangle beneath the canopy. Indeed, the next airframe in the line hasn't even got the box!

**Below** With the sun low in the west, groundcrewmen from the 335th TFS 'Chiefs' prepare 87–0200 for a night sortie. Live AIM-9s have been firmly fixed to the shoulder pylons, and the air conditioning unit for the aircraft's vast suite of avionics has been securely plugged in. Having framed the F-15E beautifully with the ground generator cord, the camouflaged technician heads in towards the built-in connecting socket beneath the Strike Eagle. The innocuous looking pod affixed immediately below the starboard intake is the navigating portion of the LANTIRN (Low Altitude Navigation and Targeting Infra-red for Night) system, the F-15E's bolt-on brain, which comes into its own after dusk. The pod consists of a Litton forward-looking infra-red (FLIR) aperture immediately below the intake, and a Texas Instruments terrain following radar. These systems, along with the Strike Eagle's own immensely capable Hughes APG-70 radar, give the pilot an outstanding view of the terrain rushing towards him in any weather, day or night

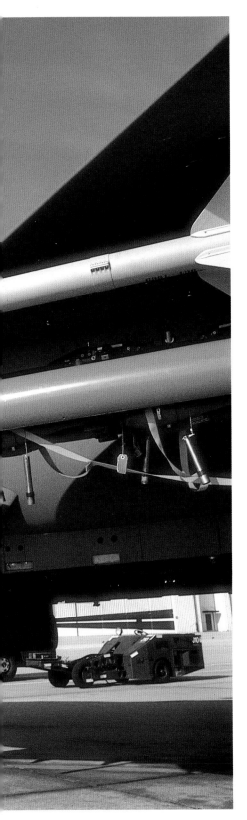

**Above** Fresh from the St Louis factory, F-15E 88–1668 has just had its high-speed refuelling receptical installed forward of the wing/fuselage join. To ensure that the modification has been carried out satisfactorily, a technician from the 336th TFS pressure checks the entire fuel-feed system of the aircraft before declaring it operational

**Left** Low angle view of F-15E 88–1686, the personal mount of the boss of the 335th TFS. Fitted below the live Sidewinder is an SUU-20 combined practice bomb/rocket dispenser, six small blue 25 lb bomblets already sitting snugly within the housing. The intensive work-ups undertaken by the 336th TFS on their new mounts paid dividends when the unit was tasked to support the coalition forces in the Gulf. Flying over 1100 sorties whilst stationed in eastern Saudi Arabia, the squadron performed most of these missions at medium to high altitude, usually at night

**Right** Brigadier General J O McFalls eases himself into the front seat of his personal F-15E. Boss of the then 4th TFW at the time of their transition from Phantom II to Strike Eagle, the Brigadier General has since been promoted to a staff job at the Pentagon

**Opposite** With its integral ladder beckoning the crew to climb aboard, 'Rocketeers' F-15E 87–0203 awaits its next sortie. The 'Rocketeers' have a crop of very experienced pilots and WSOs on the books, one of the senior personnel being ex-Vietnam Phantom II driver Lt Col Bob Gruver. His first (candid!) impressions of the Eagle went as follows: 'All the pilots love the F-15E as McDonnell Douglas spent a long time perfecting the type. The only problem with the F-4 was that it was easy to catch your sleeve on the canopy hinges when entering the cockpit! The F-15E canopy gives you virtually 360 degrees of undistorted vision, and if I want to see what's underneath me I just fly upside down!'

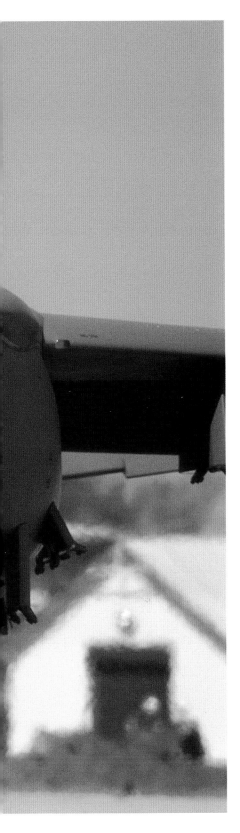

**Above** When the big boss is leading the sortie you want to make sure that all systems are operable before launch. Three pilots from the 336th TFS go 'heads down' before signalling that they are ready to taxi to the EOR check area. Led by Brigadier General McFalls, the four-ship formation will launch at 15-second intervals and then perform an inflight systems check before setting a course for the target. Maintaining radio silence until in sight of the bombing range, the quartet of F-15Es will then make a combat descent in arrowhead formation before commencing their ordnance runs on the target

**Left** Harness checked; ejection controls armed; flight controls free; flaps down and take-off trim set; canopy closed and locked; IFF (Identification friend or foe) on and radar primed; pitot heat and anti-icing on as required; warnings, cautions and circuit breakers all checked. With the pre-flight cockpit drills completed, the pilot of 88–1694 waits for clearance from the tower to 'line up 26'

**Above** Both the nose wheel steering and rudders are operated by the rudder pedals on the F-15E, although the aircraft is usually kept straight during the take-off roll by asymmetric application of the brakes as this method is far more responsive than either steering the nose wheel or toeing in the rudders. At 100 kts backward pressure is applied to the stick to raise the nose 10 degrees above the horizon, this attitude being held until the aircraft leaves the ground usually at 156 kts

**Left** Once lined up on the runway with clearance to roll from Air Traffic Control (ATC), the engines are run up to 80 per cent power for a performance check before releasing the brakes. The F-15E can be held on the brakes at up to 90 per cent thrust, but this is not a standard procedure. After brake release full throttle is set, the aircraft possessing no detents to restrict throttle movement when pushing the lever into afterburner mode. The use of the burners can reduce the take-off roll by about 3000 feet

Wearing McDonnell Douglas's standard slate grey scheme, factory-fresh 88–1695 crackles down the tarmac on full-afterburner. Having only just arrived at Seymour Johnson, this aircraft hasn't yet received its distinctive squadron stripes on its twin fins. Now re-acquainting themselves with peacetime operations after seven months of active service, the 'Rocketeers' have commenced a four-phase system to help them acclimatize to Seymour Johnson once again. The first phase has seen the F-15Es shed their almost mandatory wing tanks in order to allow the pilots to take full advantage of the aircraft's superb handling techniques. According to the unit's boss, Colonel Steven L Turner, this will allow the pilots to get back into the whole spectrum of flying the Strike Eagle. Phase two will see the crew concentrating on their air-to-air manoeuvring, both offensively and defensively, to get their G-tolerance back up to speed. The third phase concerns low-level bombing between the heights of 500 and 5000 feet. As mentioned previously, most sorties were carried out at altitudes exceeding these levels, so crews have to once again achieve proficiency in the art of low-level delivery, and its associated dangers. The final phase involves live weapons delivery at the nearby Dare County Bombing Range

During a standard training sortie departure, the gear and flaps are retracted about 16 seconds after brake release at an altitude of 100 feet. Accelerating through 250 kts, the nose of the F-15E is held at 10 degrees until 300 kts is reached, the pilot then switching off the afterburner and the aircraft settling at its optimum rate of climb of 350 kts, with the nose 10 to 15 degrees above the horizon. At Seymour Johnson the Strike Eagles usually cross the end of the runway after lift off at about 1000 feet

**Left** Maintaining a steady 300 kts at 20,000 ft above the lush Virgin Islands, a 335th TFS F-15E slowly closes on a KC-10 from the 68th AREFW. Storeless, bar a live AIM-9L round beneath the starboard wing, this aircraft has already dropped its ordnance and is about to receive the first of two top ups during its journey home. Like most other Strike Eagles present at Seymour Johnson at the time of the author's visit, this aircraft carries only the navigation pod beneath its starboard intake

**Above** From a head-on perspective, the F-15E clearly shows its 'jumboized' mid-fuselage, the bulging Dash-4 conformal fuel tanks giving the aircraft a far more rounded appearance than the comparatively lightweight F-15C. Bolt on eight CBU-71 Rockeye dispensers and the Strike Eagle looks positively obese. Heading south down the Atlantic seaboard towards NAS Roosevelt Roads, this 'Chiefs' F-15E pushes ever closer to the tanker's flying boom. The Strike Eagle/Rockeye combination proved deadly in the Gulf when both the 335th and 336th TFSs waged war against the Iraqi Republican Guard near the northern border of occupied Kuwait. According to 'Rocketeers' CO Col Turner, every system in the F-15E was thoroughly tested during *Desert Storm*, and all performed as advertised. He added that although the squadron dropped mainly Mk 82s and Mk 84s, plus cluster bombs, both the 335th and 336th TFSs achieved certification on other munitions, including laser-guided bombs (LGBs)

**Left** Tanking completed, the 'Chief' of the 'Chiefs' gently falls behind the KC-10 and reefs the F-15E away to take up a cruising position in echelon with the refueller. The unpainted square forward of the cockpit covers an automatic direction finder (ADF) aerial. Although the 336th TFS were the first to arrive in the Gulf, the 'Chiefs' of the 335th TFS were despatched to bolster the coalition ranks on 27 December 1990. Led by Lt Col Steve Pingel, the unit flew no fewer than 5000 combat hours in only 67 days during the war. As a result of this heavy workload, several of the 30 aircrew assigned to the 335th returned home to Seymour Johnson with more combat hours than total peacetime flying on the F-15E! Relying heavily on just 12 LANTIRN targeting pods (a piece of kit that many crews had used for less than a month prior to deploying), the squadron destroyed more than 400 tanks and artillery pieces in the Kuwaiti theatre of operations. 'Even though we didn't have enough pods for everyone to designate with, we force multiplied by using a dumb bomber and a smart bomber with a designator. This worked very well as our success rate with the LGBs was 75 to 80 per cent', explained Lt Col Pingel

**Above** Wearing a distinctive tricolour stripe and the drop-shadow '4th TFW' titling on the fin, this F-15E could only belong to the boss of the wing. The oldest F-15E based at Seymour Johnson, 87–0181 was also the first airframe delivered to the 4th Wing. Immediately behind the cockpit are the exit louvres for the air conditioning system. The Strike Eagle's cooling unit is considerably more powerful than that fitted in the F-15C, this modification resulting from the more complex mission avionics fitted into the two-seater

TACTICAL AIR COMMAND
SJ
AF 88 1695
SJ
4 TFW
DANGER ARRESTING HOOK

**Above** Trouble shooting in the 335th AMU hangar, Sgt Mike House (left) and Airman Tom Shahan (right) get to grips with the pitch and roll channel assembly, a crucial part of the auto flight control system. Responding to a report from the pilot who stated that the 'pitch ratio' warning light was illuminated during the aircraft's last flight, the 'groundies' have got the relevant tool kit out and commenced a thorough tweaking of the system. If the fault was not rectified the flight controls would eventually become 'sloppy' and lose responsiveness

**Left** From the oldest airframe to one of the newest. Parked up alongside '0181', a factory-fresh F-15E sits amongst aircraft it followed down the St Louis production line. With each Strike Eagle worth roughly US $50 million a piece, the total value of the hardware visible in this photograph is quite staggering

With all systems up and running, the front office of the Strike Eagle is the perfect advert for the American avionics industry. Designed from scratch to be ergonomically friendly to the crew, the cockpits are dominated by multi-purpose displays (CRTs), which have replaced many of the 1960s-vintage analogue dials. Described by the crew as 'missionized' cockpits, the displays can be optimized for air-to-ground or air-to-air missions, the set-up of the system being altered in detail by the crewmembers themselves. In this view the CRT on the left has been set up to show the Litton pod's target – a fuel bowser. The CRT on the right has a moving map image of Seymour Johnson displayed, the virtually parallel runways and taxi track showing up clearly at the bottom of the screen. The third display (the only colour CRT up front) has an artificial horizon emblazoned across it. As with the older F-15C, the cockpit of the Strike Eagle is blessed with an abundance of arm and leg room

Inside the WSO's domain. From left to right the CRT screens display: the altitude directional indicator (ADI), based on an artificial horizon display; the Hughes APG-70 radar display, optimized here in the air-to-air target acquisition mode; the Horizontal Situation Indicator (HSI), which shows the position of the F-15E in relation to predetermined navigation waypoints; and lastly the trick moving map image generated by the Tactical Situation Display (TSD) unit. Any of these images can be shuffled from screen to screen by the WSO using two Hands on Throttle and Stick (HOTAS) controllers. Information can also be quickly passed from the back seat forward, and vice versa. Tucked unobtrusively beneath the CRTs are a small set of primary flight instruments, which combine with the fully operable joystick to give the back-seater the option to fly the F-15E should the pilot become incapacitated. Many of the 4th TFW's WSOs are in fact pilot-rated on the Strike Eagle

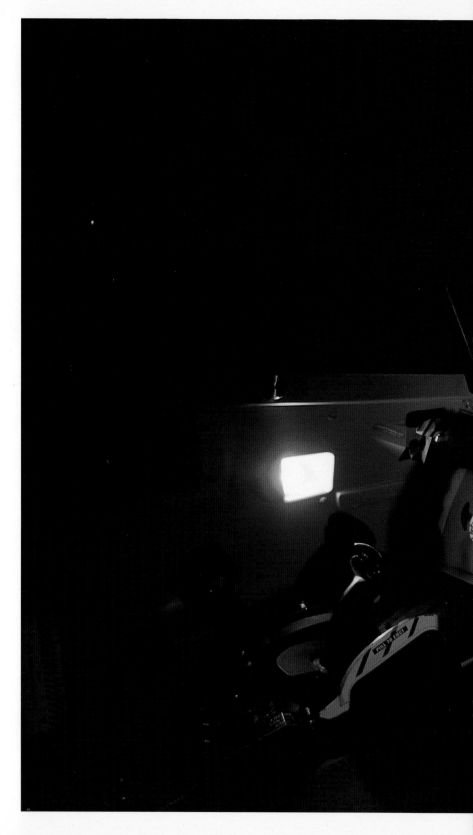

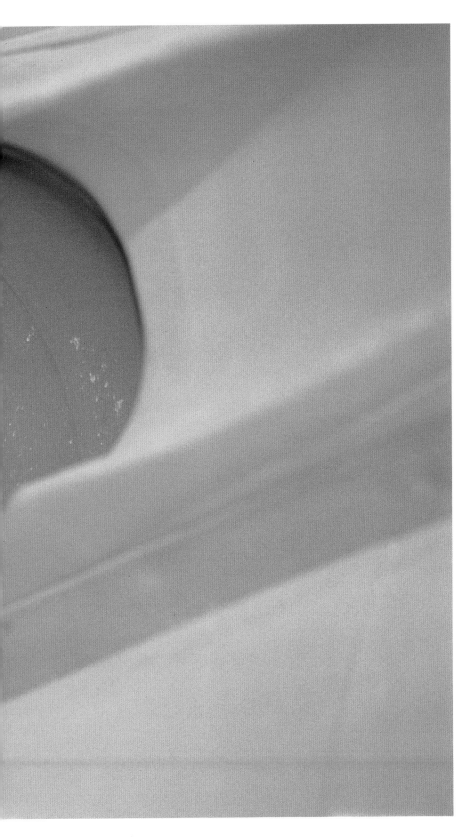

**Above** Hidden away inside the nose wheel housing is this little grey box, technically referred to as the Built-in Test Equipment Panel, or BITE for short. If there is a snag with the aircraft, the relevant numbered window will turn orange. To isolate the problem all the groundcrew then have to do is cross-reference the number with the menu printed on the black strip immediately below the BITE. By the looks of this panel, the boys from the AMU are in for a busy day with this F-15E

**Left** As with the fighter optimized F-15A/C, the Strike Eagle carries an M61A1 Vulcan 20 mm cannon internally just behind the starboard intake. A tried and tested weapon, the cannon is fed from a 940-round magazine, housed immediately below the spine-mounted airbrake

The complex 'turkey feathers' of the
F-15E are identical to those fitted to
earlier Eagles. Powered by either the
Pratt & Whitney F100-PW-220 or the
General Electric F110, the F-15E has a
total thrust capability close to
50,000 lbs. Both engines have been
drastically developed since their
early service days to increase the
Strike Eagle's overall operability, the
F100, for example, being designed to
run for 4000 hours (nine years of use)
before its high-pressure compressor,
combustor and high-pressure turbine
need to be inspected. Added to that,
the complex afterburner assembly
has also been cleared by Pratt &
Whitney for 1200 hours of service
between inspection and
refurbishment

**Above** Sheltering from the harsh sun, '1668 is liberally festooned with protective covers, and their associated red 'bunting', inside one of the AMU hangars. Just as the 'Rocketeers' indulge in colour co-ordinated ejection seat covers, the 'Chiefs' also adorn the headrests of their McDonnell Douglas ACES II 'thrones' with appropriately tailored garments

**Left** A gaping hole marks the spot where a faulty black box once lived in the forward avionics bay of this aircraft. Removed for detailed servicing by the 335th AMU, a replacement unit will soon be slotted back into place and airframe 88–1668 restored to the operational ramp

**Above** A 'Rocketeers' F-15E. As the sun sets, the E's night vision FLIR systems provide for round the clock, all-weather operations. This Eagle never sleeps

**Left** 'I'm sure I left my spanner in here some place?' Wearing specially padded slippers and a well-used white overall, a technician from the 336th AMU goes about his business in the cool of a typically fine North Carolina evening. Inspections of the multi-petalled afterburner nozzles are performed by the respective squadron AMUs at regular intervals, the mechanics looking for warped or separating plates within the overall structure

Preparing for a night bombing sortie, the groundcrew have unlatched the nose avionics bay door to check that all is well on 88–1670 before declaring the aircraft fit for flight. Besides the mandatory seat covers, this Strike Eagle also wears a yellow LANTIRN sensor protector

A new breed of USAF pilot is being trained to fly the F-15E, and former F-4 driver Captain Mike Stansbury is one of them. Now performing a truly multi-role mission, the pilot of the Strike Eagle operates an aircraft that can function as either a fighter or a bomber, the man 'up front' having to make sure that he is proficient at both tasks. This has led to some problems as crews find it difficult to judge when to come out of air-to-air mode and recommence their ground attack profile. However, the luxury of a dedicated escort on low-level penetration sorties solves this problem immediately, a tactical factor borne out in the recent Gulf War

**Above** F-15E 88–1686 belongs to the boss of the 335th TFS, Lt Col Steve Pingel, and is one of three Strike Eagles that wears the traditional commander's drop-shadow 'SJ' code on its twin fins. Soon to carry the CO skyward, this aircraft has been loaded up with a pair of SUU-20 bomb/rocket dispensers and two live AIM-9s. The overall mission radius on this sortie must be a small one as the almost mandatory 610 US gal centreline tank is conspicuous by its absence

**Right** Outside of SAC, nose art rarely appears on frontline USAF aircraft, unless of course that aircraft happens to be the wing commander's personal jet. Regularly flown by Col Hal M Hornburg, 87–0181 has been christened 'Spirit of Goldsboro', mirroring the 4th Wing's close associations with this famous city

**Above** The loading of weapons is an art form that takes months to perfect. Different aircraft pose different problems, squadron armourers having to adapt to the high wing of the F-15E compared to the low wing of the F-4E. The grouping of much of the ordnance down the centreline of the Strike Eagle leaves little room for manoeuvre with a laden 'jammer', especially when you've got a pair of eye-wateringly expensive LANTIRN pods blocking your progress. To ensure that the aircraft will be ready for the specified time of departure, the 'rad techs' have commenced priming 87–0200's avionics whilst the armourers continue to work down at ramp level. Somewhere along the line this Strike Eagle has picked up an appropriately coloured wheel hub, which is most definitely non-standard issue!

**Left** Besieged by live Sparrows, Sidewinders and Rockeyes, 88–1695 prepares to be weighed down with ordnance prior to commencing a moonless bombing sortie. The F-15E possesses a theoretical maximum of 18 ordnance attachment points, excluding the plumbed centreline position, which is usually reserved for the external tank

Welcome to the 335th Chie[f]

World's lea[d]

MIG killers
to date

**Above** The envy of all his squadron mates, Captain George H Sewell III of the 336th TFS 'flies' this appropriately registered automobile when he's not zooming around the skies in his Strike Eagle

**Left** Forever in fighters, the 335th TFS's proud history is graphically illustrated by this huge wall mural inside the entrance of the squadron HQ. Due to a lack of trade in the Middle East, the 335th's MiG tally still remains at 218

# 'Light' Metal

In amongst the tactically painted Phantom IIs, Strike Eagles and Extenders lurks a trio of Northrop T-38A Talons, fighting for recognition on the sprawling Seymour Johnson ramp. Wearing the markings of the 12th Flying Training Wing (FTW), these aircraft serve in North Carolina all year round supporting SAC's Accelerated Co-Pilot Enrichment Program for KC-10 right-seaters

**Above** Talon 14947 is tugged from its overnight shelter out onto the detachment's small ramp at the north west corner of the 4th Wing's line. Emphasizing the det's self-sufficiency, even the tow-tractor belongs to Air Training Command (ATC), and was flown in specially from the 12th FTW's home in Texas. A total of eight crew are assigned to run Operating Location Foxtrot (OLF), as the Seymour Johnson 'squadronette' is known. This number consists of three instructor pilots and five maintenance technicians

**Right** Whilst the KC-10 co-pilot commences his instrument checks in the front seat, the instructor is helped on with his straps by the 'camouflaged' plane captain. As with all training aircraft, the rescue markings are clearly visible on this T-38 against the traditional ATC gloss white scheme

**Above** The pilot signals that number one engine has successfully ignited and the groundcrewman responds by giving him the signal to light the second General Electric J85-GE-5. Developing 3950 lbs of thrust a piece, the diminutive (but excessively noisy) J85s have proven to be extremely robust powerplants, giving the Talon a true supersonic capability unmatched by any other trainer in its class. In service for close on to 30 years now, the Talon has compiled a safety record unparalleled by other USAF aircraft that can achieve supersonic performance

**Right** Maintained in spotless condition, 14947 belies its advancing age, having been built by Northrop in 1971. A total of 73 T-38s are controlled by the 12th FTW, this burgeoning fleet of airframes being split into three maintenance flights. Marked with a black number 2 on the trailing edge of the fin, this particular T-38 is assigned to the second maintenance flight

With both engines fully spooled up, the crew continue their heads down check of the instruments before signalling for the right wheel chock to be removed

**Above** Ground navigation is also practised on these sorties as the Talon crew have to head southward towards runway 26 from their ramp, via the parallel taxyway that runs the whole length of the fighter flightline. The pilot then turns left past the transient aircraft ramp and the trees that surround the control tower, before tracking through the tanker ramp and past the 171st FIS's alert barns. Only the EOR check area then remains between the Talon and the runway holding point!

**Left** Brakes off, 14947 commences its long journey to the holding point of runway 26. The mission of the 12th FTW's OLF is to provide supplemental training for KC-10 co-pilots upgrading to aircraft commander level. Once pilots regain currency on the T-38, they fly team navigation sorties to various stateside bases including Pope, Myrtle Beach, Langley and Shaw, giving them valuable first-pilot experience, with an emphasis on cross-country flying and landing away from the base

**Left** Flashing past a parked KC-10A parked in the distance, the 'trainee pilot' of '947 performs a touch and go on the long black top. A pilot under instruction will normally make eight to ten sorties with a qualified jock in the back seat before going solo during the major transition from co-pilot to commander

**Above** Keeping the nose up before opening the throttle, the pilot rolls down the runway. Besides operating the Seymour Johnson OLF, the 12th FTW also maintains a small det at Malmstrom AFB, Montana, supporting the KC-135R Stratotanker co-pilots of the 301st Air Refueling Wing

# Vital Extender

Virtually surrounded by General Electric CF6-50C2 turbofan engines, a drab KC-10 Extender bakes in the mid-afternoon sun. The newly created 4th Wing is unique in the Air Force as it has merged the tanker and fighter forces into a single composite structure, deactivating the 68th ARW in the process. Commencing on 22 April 1991, all aerial assets at the base are now controlled by the ex-boss of the 4th TFW, Colonel Hal M Hornburg. 'I know these changes will enhance our capability because they better organize us for wartime operations', the Colonel stated. Each department at Seymour Johnson now falls under the control of one of four groups. The 4th Operations Group controls the three F-15E squadrons, the two KC-10 units, and an operations squadron. The 4th Logistics Group consists of all the maintenance units and supply and transportation squadrons. The other organizations established at Seymour Johnson are the 4th Support Group and the 4th Medical Group. Designed to increase the Air Force's ability to rapidly perform 'out of theatre' operations, the composite wing theory is also being applied to units at Pope AFB, North Carolina, Mountain Home AFB, Idaho, and Davis-Monthan AFB, Arizona

**Above** As can be clearly seen from this low angle shot, the paint scheme worn by most KC-10s is one of extreme contrast, the overall charcoal grey dominating the fuselage. The original light grey applied by McDonnell Douglas at its Long Beach facility still remains on the underbelly, and is maintained with as glossy a finish as possible to try and offset the drag caused by the 'rough' upper surfaces. This particular machine, 87–0123 'Carolina Dream', is having its fuel feed pipe checked out

**Left** A smoky KC-135A provides a blast from the past as it comes in on long finals. Flown by the former 68th ARW for 22 years, the last KC-135 departed Seymour Johnson for fresh Air National Guard pastures in October 1985. The wing itself dated back to August 1941 when it served as a reconnaissance and bombardment outfit operating such classics as the Douglas A-20 Havoc, Boeing B-17 and B-29, Consolidated B-24 Liberator, Lockheed P-38 Lightning, Bell P-39 Airacobra and the North American P-51 Mustang. Tasked with the new role of air-to-air refuelling in support of SAC's burgeoning bomber force, the now-defunct wing re-equipped with KC-97Es in 1953, before trading up to Stratotankers (and engulfing the 911th ARS in the process) ten years later

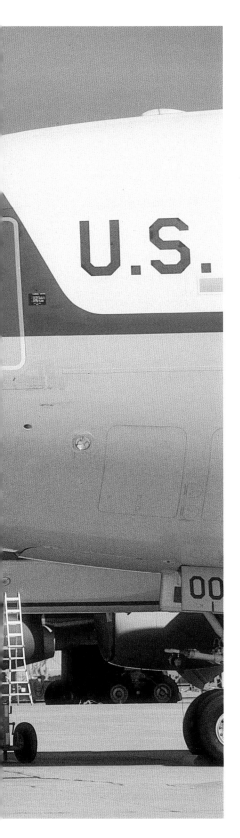

**Above** Shot through an ultra-wide angle lens, the tailplane of 'Carolina Dream' takes on massive proportions. The full-span elevators on each tailplane are powered by Bertea actuators which give the pilot longitudinal and directional control. The small circle to the right of the base of the flying boom is the fuselage cut-out for the probe and drogue reel unit, the KC-10 storing 80 feet of hose in a special housing just forward of the boom operator's position

**Left** Nose art has flourished on SAC assets over the past decade, the detail of some of the designs being quite breathtaking. The motifs worn by the 20-strong Extender force at Seymour Johnson are definitely amongst the most impressive to be seen in the SAC ranks. Nicknamed 'Great White' for obvious reasons, KC-10A 83–0077 is one of a pair of glossy Extenders on the books with the 4th Wing, and judging by the state of the paint, it will not be too long before it too trades in its 'SAC blue' for charcoal grey

**Above** 'Carolina Dream' improves its tan on the 4th Wing tanker ramp. Along with most other SAC refuelling assets, the wing was heavily involved in supporting coalition assets in the Gulf from August 1990 onwards. Participating virtually from the word go, the tankers assisted 22 F-15Es from the 336th when they headed east from Seymour Johnson to Thrumrait AB, Oman, on 9 August 1990

**Right** Departing on yet another sortie, 82–0192 rotates its gear and commences its climb away from the base. This particular airframe is the oldest KC-10A at Seymour Johnson, most other Extenders being of fiscal year 1986/87 vintage

**Above** Leading slats deployed and double-slotted flaps extended, 'Peace Maker' gently climbs away from runway 26. The pilot is already 'cleaning up' the undercarriage gear and he will soon throttle back the engines to conserve fuel. No fewer than seven unpressurized fuel bladder cells are fitted beneath the cargo loading floor in a KC-10, three forward of the wing and four aft. Totally interconnected with the aircraft's integral wing tanks, the bladders are protected by keel beams and energy-absorbing material

**Left** Pre-flight checks before the early morning mission to refuel 334th TFS F-4Es and 335th TFS F-15Es, en route to the Caribbean. Whilst RAF exchange officer Flt Lt Philip Curr tweaks the switches on the comms panel, co-pilot 1st Lt Todd Helgeson sets the take-off speed 'bugs' around the outside of the airspeed indicator. As can be seen from this shot, the cockpit lay-out of a KC-10A is basically similar to that built into its civilian brother, the DC-10 Series 30CF

Cruising over the Caribbean at 23,000 feet and maintaining 350 kts, 'Peace Maker' overflies the Bahamas. Although wearing a Union Jack on his left shoulder, co-pilot Helgeson is most definitely an American! The patch actually belongs to Flt Lt Curr, an experienced tanker pilot who, previous to his two-and-a-half-year exchange with the 68th, had served for five years on Victor K.2s with No 55 Sqn at RAF Marham. Once his exchange is completed he will return to the UK and take up a tanker commander posting on Tristar K.1s with No 216 Sqn at RAF Brize Norton. Just as British pilots and navigators 'go west' at regular intervals, their USAF equivalents head east to serve with the RAF's diverse tanker force also

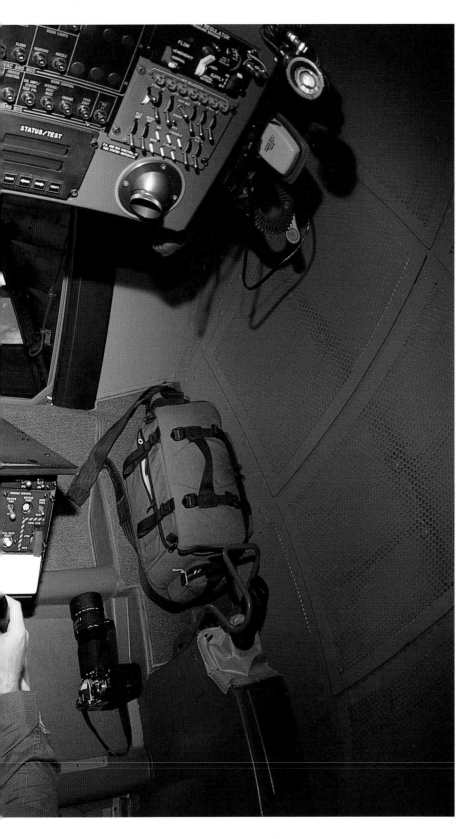

Even a fisheye lens can't make the boom operator's position look spacious. Here, Tech Sgt Don Cox delivers fuel to a 334th TFS F-4E en route to Puerto Rico. Purpose-built for the Aerial Refueling Officer (ARO), as he is officially known, the station is a vast improvement on the prone position offered to the KC-135 boomer. The ARO 'flies' the McDonnell Douglas Aerial Refueling Boom (AARB) through a 'fly-by-wire' control system which links the elevator and dual rudders. The boomer also has a 'trick' piece of kit, manufactured by Sperry, to help ease his life, the Built In Test (BIT) facility sensing whether the AARB is positioned correctly, telescoping according to control inputs, and whether there is available hydraulic pressure on hand to pump the fuel. Just as the crew up front pre-flight the KC-10 before launch, the boomer too can check his systems out before commencing the sortie using the Sperry BIT

**Above** The boomer has an array of mirrors positioned to widen his horizon, the pair above and below the rear window giving him an unobstructed view of the approaching aircraft when it is directly behind the Extender, and above the angle of vision through the window. Sideways looking mirrors are mounted in the floor between the boomer's legs. A total of six pumps are fitted in the KC-10, which give a maximum flow rate of 1500 US gallons per minute! However, when topping up a thirsty F-15E only one or two pumps need be activated, saving the 'six pack' for a thirsty C-5 or fellow KC-10

**Right** Tanks topped up, the CO of the 335th TFS drops back from the tanker and heads northward, bound for Seymour Johnson. During the *Caribbean Eagle II* sortie, the F-4s and F-15s utilized the pair of KC-10s both before and after their respective bombing runs, thus increasing their radius of action appreciably

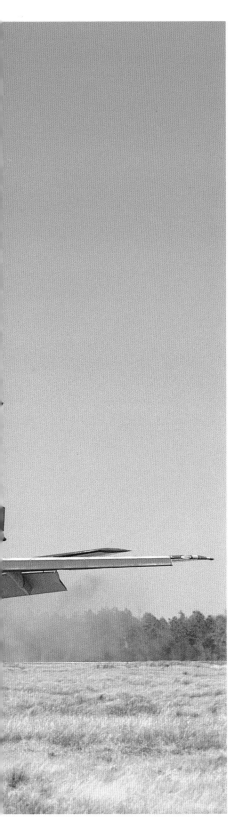

**Left and above** Gliding down the approach to runway 26, 'Peace Maker' closes in on the tarmac at 129 kts, the pilot keeping 5 kts 'up his sleeve' for gust response. From this angle, the single-strut central undercarriage leg is clearly visible, this unique device being a distinguising feature of the McDonnell Douglas design

**Right** Mission accomplished! One of two KC-10s that took part in *Caribbean Eagle II* over Puerto Rico, 'Peace Maker' was crewed on this occasion by members of the 911th Air Refueling Squadron (ARS), one of two full-time units in the wing (the other one being the 344th ARS). Pictured here from left to right are Tech Sgt Don Cox, boom operator; Flt Lt Philip Curr (RAF exchange), aircraft commander; Tech Sgt Julio Inocencio, flight engineer; SM Sgt Charles Gurkin, boom-operator; and First Lt Todd Helgeson, co-pilot. The other KC-10 was crewed by reservists from the 434th ARS, this unit operating side by side with its full-time sister squadrons helping to ensure high utilization of the aircraft and to keep frontline crew exhaustion to a minimum. This 'associate' programme has been in operation throughout SAC's KC-10 force since the Extender first entered service in late 1981

**Left** The small symbol above the tail-mounted GE CF6 is the wing's stylized Wright Flyer emblem, which denotes the closeness of Seymour Johnson and Kitty Hawk. Clearly visible on 'Great White', this badge is worn in black on all 4th Wing KC-10s. Unlike its drab wing mates, 83–0077 retains bare metal leading edges to the wing, fin and engine intake areas

**Above** The traditional star-spangled SAC stripe splits the badges of the 434th ARS and the 68th ARW

The KC-10 is perhaps the most expensive 'canvas' ever used in North Carolina! The murals with a 'heavy metal' bent are all the handiwork of a single artist who goes by the name of Rooney

# Base Bits

Inside the mobile radar approach control (RAPCON), Tec Sgt Abernathy and Snr Airman Mays look after the Seymour Johnson Special Rules Airspace. With a 60-mile range, and covering airspace up to an altitude of 10,000 feet, the base controllers also provide approach control for four nearby civilian airports

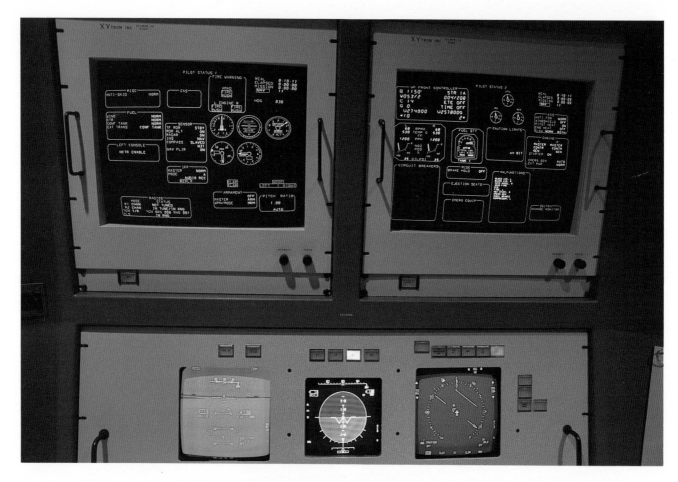

**Above** The F-15E flight simulator at Seymour Johnson is controlled by Doyle Payne of Loral Defense Systems, along with Jerry McCullough and Lance Whitmore. The panel shown here allows the instructor to monitor the cockpit instruments. Top left is 'Pilot Status 1' with basic flight instruments and switches; 'Pilot Status 2' (top right) covers emergency situations such as fires, hydraulic failures, generator failures and fuel problems. The bottom row from left to right comprises a head-up display (HUD) showing the picture from the NAV FLIR (navigational forward looking infrared) with pitch and steering information. In the middle is the ADI (attitude directional indicator). This displays calculated airspeed and heading attitude, whilst the final monitor shows the heading and position of the aircraft relative to navigation aids

**Right** CRT number seven on the instructor's display panel describes an 'AZARR TWO' procedural departure from runway three at Luke AFB, Arizona. A pilot can taxi out and take-off from virtually any facility in the USAF using these simulators, and, conversely, he can also recover to any base he wishes

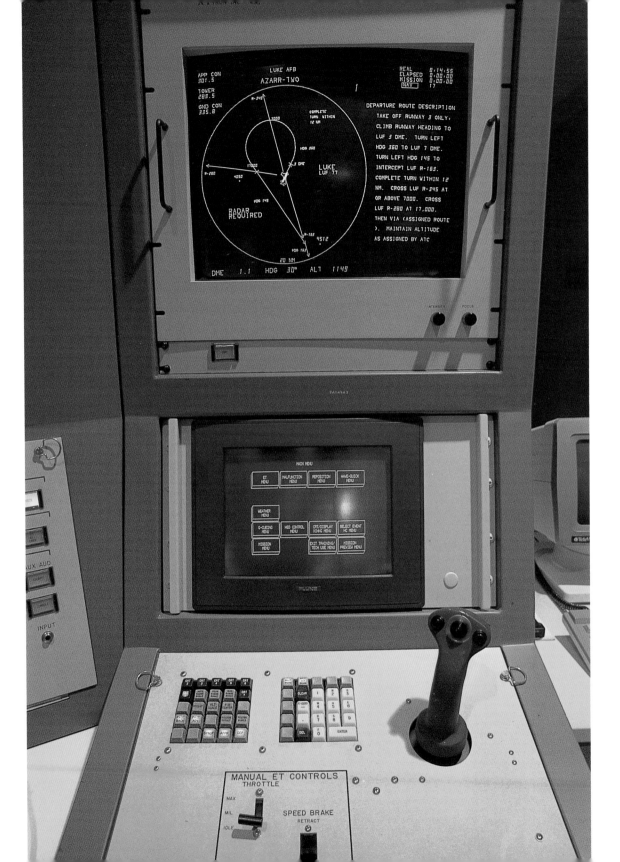

**Above** The Weapons Systems Officer display panel. The WSO status screens are at the top. Along the bottom are the ADI, air-to-air radar display, Horizontal Situation Indicator (HSI) and Tactical Situation Display (TSD). The TSD is a moving map which shows exactly where the aircraft is in relation to geographical features, the system being constantly updated through inputs from the radar. Once in a position to drop their ordnance, the crew can slave their bolt-on targetting pod to the TSD for ultra-accurate weapons delivery

**Right** This is the Problem Control Panel. From here the instructor can introduce problems or emergency situations during the simulated flight in order to monitor how the pilot reacts. In this instance, the instructor has disabled the pilot's head-up display, and he has responded by activating the emergency back-up system. As can be seen from the keypad menus, all manner of disasters can befall the budding Strike Eagle driver in the comfort of the simulator building

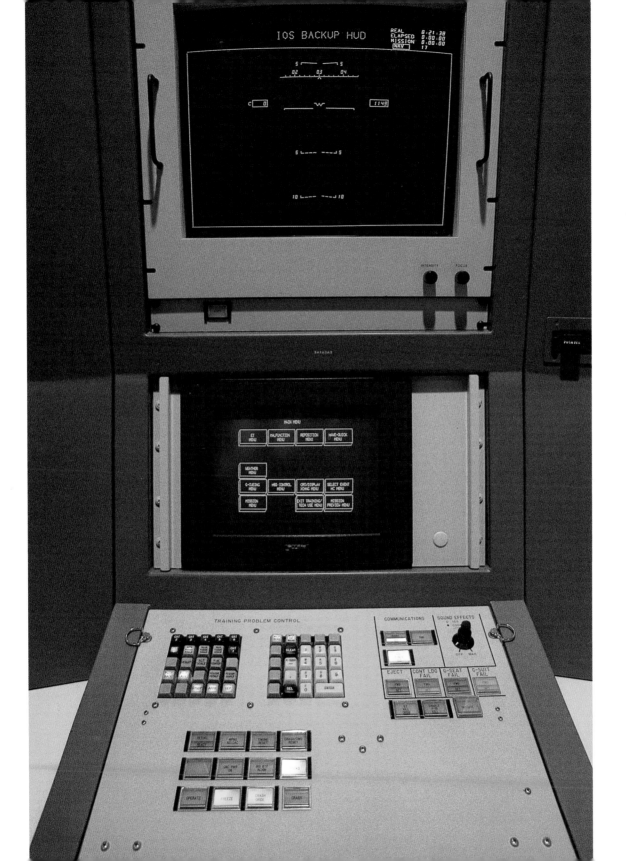

**Above** Across the well nurtured lawn from the F-105 is this rather weathered F-4C Phantom II, nicknamed 'Jeanie'. Built in 1964 as part of the final batch of 275 Charlie models, 63–0770 never actually served with the wing. It was, however, flown in Vietnam by General Robert F Russ, current commander of TAC, and an ex-boss of the 4th TFW. The Phantom II eventually arrived in North Carolina in 1987 after being retired by the 123rd Fighter Interceptor Squadron (FIS), Oregon Air Guard

**Left** Splitting the firs outside the headquarters of the 4th Tactical Wing is this veteran Republic F-105D Thunderchief, which wears a South-east Asian camouflage scheme and tricolour squadron stripes on the fin. Built in 1961 as part of Contract AF33 (600)-40838, Project 90, for 180 aircraft, F-105D 61–0056 saw active service with the wing in the early 1960s. Thunderchiefs graced the Seymour Johnson ramp from 1959 to 1966

Things have progressed quite a way since the 4th TFW, or Fighter Interceptor Wing as they were then known, was despatched to Korea with their North American F-86A Sabres in November 1950. Over the next three years the wing would account for no fewer than 502 enemy aircraft destroyed. This veteran F-86F is finished in the markings of MiG ace Captain Lonnie Moore, a crack pilot from the 335th FIS. The 34th jet ace of the Korean War, Captain Moore accounted for nine MiG-15s and a single Lavochkin LA-9 during his tour. As a tribute to his wife and son, Captain Moore adorned his Sabre with the names 'Margie' and 'Billie' on either side of the aircraft's fuselage

# Heraldry

Just as the frontline units proudly wear squadron colours on their overalls, so too do the Air National Guard crews. The 171st FIS motif is not worn on squadron aircraft, the Aztec Indian-inspired design finding a home only on the shoulders of the aircrew. The unofficial 'F-4 Six Pack' design does, however, reflect the traditional 'Michigan checkers'. Now a collector's item, this badge has been altered to better reflect the unit's recent re-equipment with the F-16A

The unit badges of the 4th Wing are amongst the most famous insignia worn by any TAC-gained outfit. As can be seen from these close-up shots, the badges themselves are applied to the airframe as decals by squadron maintainers, usually following a major overhaul or, in the case of the Strike Eagle, after having arrived fresh from the factory

**Left** Opposing the unit badge on the right intake of each 4th TW aircraft is the highly-stylized wing emblem. The flame streaming from the arrow symbolizes the jet propulsion of the unit's aircraft, whilst the stripes of the shield relate to the three squadrons within the original 4th TFW

**Below** Along with the wing badge, each F-15E carries a 'screaming eagle' on the inside of the twin fins, this motif actually being applied as a finishing touch at the McDonnell Douglas paint shop in St Louis. The bullet fairing on top of the fin houses electronic countermeasures (ECM) jammers, which are part of the awesome Northrop ALQ-135 system. The small white-capped blister fairing immediately below the jammer is also tied in with the aircraft's Tactical Electronic Warfare System (TEWS), housing a 'rear facing circularly polarized planar spiral aerial'. Built by Loral, and designated the ALR-56, the system actively seeks out and classifies hostile radar emissions, jamming them automatically according to their perceived threat. The small fairing beneath the ALR-56 contains a high intensity anti-collision beacon

**Above left** The setting sun picks out all the fine panelling detail on the port fin of a 336th TFS F-15E. The twin rudders on the Strike Eagle are driven by small Ronson rotary hydraulic motors

**Above right** When squadrons re-equip with new aircraft, standard USAF policy is to try and place airframes from the same production batch with one unit. As a result, any post-production modifications and updates that take place can then be easily retrofitted to the entire squadron

Every flying outfit at Seymour Johnson has a shoulder patch, even the T-38 ACE detachment. Proudly worn by many KC-10 right-seaters, the patch symbolizes a job well done amongst the young SAC crews